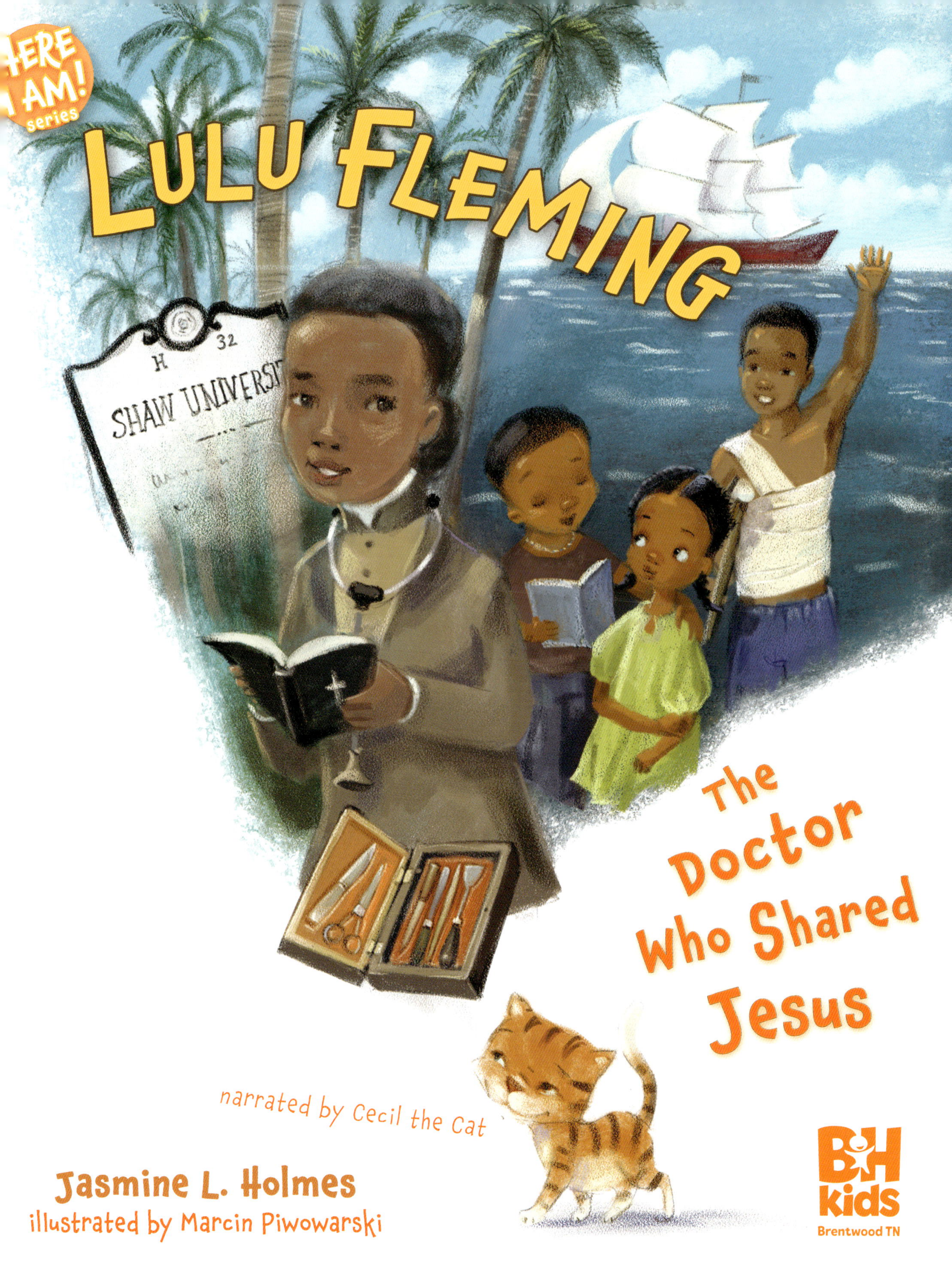
HERE I AM! series
LULU FLEMING
H 32
SHAW UNIVERSIT
The Doctor Who Shared Jesus
narrated by Cecil the Cat
Jasmine L. Holmes
illustrated by Marcin Piwowarski
B&H kids
Brentwood TN

For Daddy, the teller of epic bedtime stories,
& Mama, my first and best teacher

Look through the book to find all the images from the cover! Find the ship, the Shaw University sign, palm trees, a boy with a blue book, a girl in a green shirt, a man with a bandage, a medical kit, Cecil the Cat, and Lulu holding her Bible.

Published by B&H Publishing Group, Brentwood, Tennessee

978-1-4300-9642-9

Dewey Decimal Classification: CB
Subject Heading: FLEMING, LULU \ MISSIONARIES \
WOMEN MISSIONARIES
Printed in Shenzhen, Guangdong, China, February 2024
1 2 3 4 5 6 · 28 27 26 25 24

Hi, friend!

My name is Cecil the Cat, and I am going to share a very special story with you about my friend Dr. Louise Cecilia Fleming. You can call her Lulu.

Lulu's story starts the same way all stories do—long before she was born. Her grandfather was a young man in a beautiful country called **the Congo** when slave traders captured him and brought him on a long, frightening journey to America.

COAST OF THE CONGO

Slave traders were people who kidnapped other people and then sold them for money. Lulu's grandfather was captured because he had brown skin, and the slave traders thought he wasn't worthy of respect. This might sound very mean to you, and it should!

Brown-skinned people who came from the continent of Africa were sometimes called "Black," while lighter-skinned people who came from Europe were sometimes called "White."

God made all kinds of people to show His creativity and love, but sometimes, one group of people wrongly thinks that their differences make them better than other people.

Because Lulu's grandfather was captured, Lulu was born into slavery in a small town in Florida. Children with brown skin like Lulu, or Black children, were not allowed to learn how to read or write. They had to work in harsh conditions with no pay.

Lulu was not allowed to see her parents while they worked from sunup to sundown. She knew there was always a chance that her parents could be taken away from her by her slave traders.

Lulu's father fought against slavery in something called the Civil War.

The Civil War was a fight between the northern and southern states in America.

Part of the reason for the war was to free people like Lulu and her parents from slavery.

After the war, Lulu's family was **finally free.** This freedom did not erase the ugly ideas about people with brown skin.

But freedom did mean that Lulu could make her own choices about her future. Lulu got to go to school for the first time! She learned alongside many other children who had never been allowed to go to school because of the color of their skin.

Some people might think school is boring. But to Lulu, it was an amazing place she could learn about reading, writing, math, and all about the world. At school, **Lulu met Jesus.**

No, Jesus didn't walk into her classroom and introduce Himself. Lulu met Jesus the same way you could meet Him: **through reading His Word,** the Bible, for the very first time.

Many times, children who grew up enslaved weren't allowed to learn much about the Bible. Slaveholders were afraid they'd learn about people like Moses, who led the Israelites to freedom!

You see, even though Lulu was free now, people still viewed her as *less than* because she was Black.

Remember, ending slavery did not end those ugly thoughts about Black people. In fact, many people tried to twist God's Word to defend those thoughts.

But in the Bible, Lulu saw that she was precious to God and that He had made her skin on purpose to show His creativity and love. She learned that all people have dignity: God made them worthy of honor and respect.

Genesis 1:27 says, "So God created man in his own image; he created him in the image of God; he created them male and female."

Lulu's teachers noticed that she was very bright and arranged for her to continue her education at Shaw University. There, she became a teacher and made it her life's mission to tell people about her creative God.

After a few years of teaching Black students in Florida, Lulu decided to teach children in **the Congo—** the place from which her grandfather had been stolen.

In the Bible, Lulu read all about God's care for little children just like the ones she felt called to teach.

Lulu's journey across the ocean was not easy. She traveled thousands of miles by boat with other missionaries, but she was the only Black missionary. It was very brave of Lulu to travel so far from home on her own!

Lulu was the first Black missionary to travel with the Woman's American Baptist Foreign Missionary Society to another country to share about Jesus.

Many other Black women like Maria Fearing, Lucy Sheppard, and Althea Edmiston were missionaries in the Congo, but they weren't serving with Lulu.

Cats can live in America, the Congo, and on boats like the one Lulu traveled on!

In the Congo, a cruel leader named King Leopold II had the same ugly ideas about people with brown skin as the men who had captured Lulu's grandfather all those years ago.

The king put the Congolese people to work in cruel and violent ways that made Lulu very sad.

By going to the Congo, Lulu was once again in a country where Black people were enslaved and forced to work without pay. She dared to stand up to the same mean ideas she had faced in her home country.

Lulu set up a school for Congolese children. She taught young girls and boys about Jesus and about reading, writing, and math—the knowledge that had been hidden from her as a young girl.

She taught the children that **God made their skin** and He loved it. Each child was a special, creative part of God's plan and had dignity, just like Lulu.

Lulu helped some students go to her old school in America, Shaw University.

A few years later, Lulu got sick—but she didn't have a doctor! She realized that the people in the Congo needed a doctor. Since she had to return to America to get better, she decided to be trained to become a doctor herself.

Lulu was the first Black woman to attend her college. Not many women or Black people went to college in those days!

Eventually, Lulu made the long trip back to the Congo. She filled the people's hearts with **God's truth,** their heads with knowledge, and their bodies with care.

Lulu loved people in every way she could. She taught in the school and looked after sick Congolese people.

She helped people heal and even taught others basic medical skills so that the Congolese people would always be able to get the care they needed.

Most of all, she never stopped teaching women, men, girls, and boys about Jesus.

Because Lulu worked with very sick people every day, she knew she could catch a dangerous disease. Still, Lulu **didn't stop serving** the Congolese people.

Lulu became a doctor, or physician, to help sick people. Did you know that the Bible calls Jesus the Great Physician?

One day, Lulu got very sick. She grew so weak and tired that she had to teach children from a hammock. Lulu loved and cared for them until she had nothing more to give.

Lulu wanted to stay in the Congo more than anything, but her sickness forced her to go back to America. She wanted with all her heart to return to the people of the Congo.

Lulu is in heaven now. No doubt, she is praising God and talking about His goodness there just like she did in America and in the Congo.

Lulu treated the people of the Congo with the love of Jesus, teaching them about God and the beautiful world and people He made. She lived a life beyond her grandfather's **wildest dreams.**

God's plans for Lulu were bigger than the slave traders could ever imagine. And Lulu had God-sized dreams for the children of **the Congo** too.